# Contents

# Guess who?

A hen!

The hen sits on her eggs to keep them warm.

She gets up now and then to turn her eggs over.

**Tap! tap! tap!**

After 21 days a tiny Tap! Tap! Tap! comes from inside the eggs.

8

Cracks appear on the shells and out hatch ...

# Hello chicks!

The chicks open their eyes and dry off.

They are covered all over with soft down.

# Into the wide world

Soon the fuzzy, **fluffy** chicks go for their first walk.

seeds to eat

# From chick to chicken

When the chicks are a month old they begin to grow feathers.

Young male chickens are called cockerels.
Young female chickens are called pullets.

cockerel

pullet

# Roaming free

During the day, the chickens walk and **Squawk** around the farm.

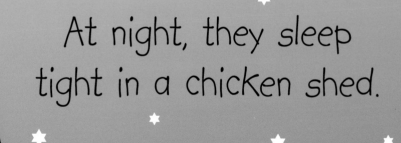

At night, they sleep
tight in a chicken shed.

# Eggs for eating

If female chickens are kept apart from male chickens, their eggs will not grow into chicks.

If they all live together,
their eggs will hatch into ...

# Count the chicks

... Lots of new chicks!

# Index

The end

## Notes for adults

The **Life as a . . .** series looks at the life cycles of familiar animals and plants, introducing the young child to the concept of change over time. There are four titles in the series and, when used together, they will enable comparison of similarities and differences between life cycles. The key curriculum early learning goals relevant to this series are:

*Knowledge and understanding of the world*
 – find out about, and identify, some features of living things that the young child observes
 – ask questions about why things happen
 – differentiate between past and present.

This book takes the reader on a circular journey from the beginning of a chicken's life as an egg, through its developmental stages (including where the chicken lives and what it needs to grow), to maturity and reproduction. The book will help children extend their vocabulary, as they will hear new words such as *down* (for the chicks' fluffy coats), *pullet* and *cockerel*. You might like to introduce the word *comb* when looking at the picture of the cockerel. The book explains that if pullets are kept apart from cockerels, their eggs will not grow into chicks. It may be helpful for young readers if you emphasize that the eggs we eat are the type that will never grow into chicks.

### Additional information about chickens

Chickens are domestic birds – this means that they are kept and bred by humans for eating. There are approximately 150 different breeds of chicken in the world today. All chickens are descended from a type of pheasant found in the jungles of Southeast Asia. Chickens were first domesticated about 8000 years ago. A hen can lay about 250 eggs a year.

### Follow-up activities

• Visit a children's farm to observe hens and chicks, pullets and cockerels.
• Hard-boil an egg and paint its shell.
• Make a model of a chicken using different materials such as clay or plasticine.